I0845070

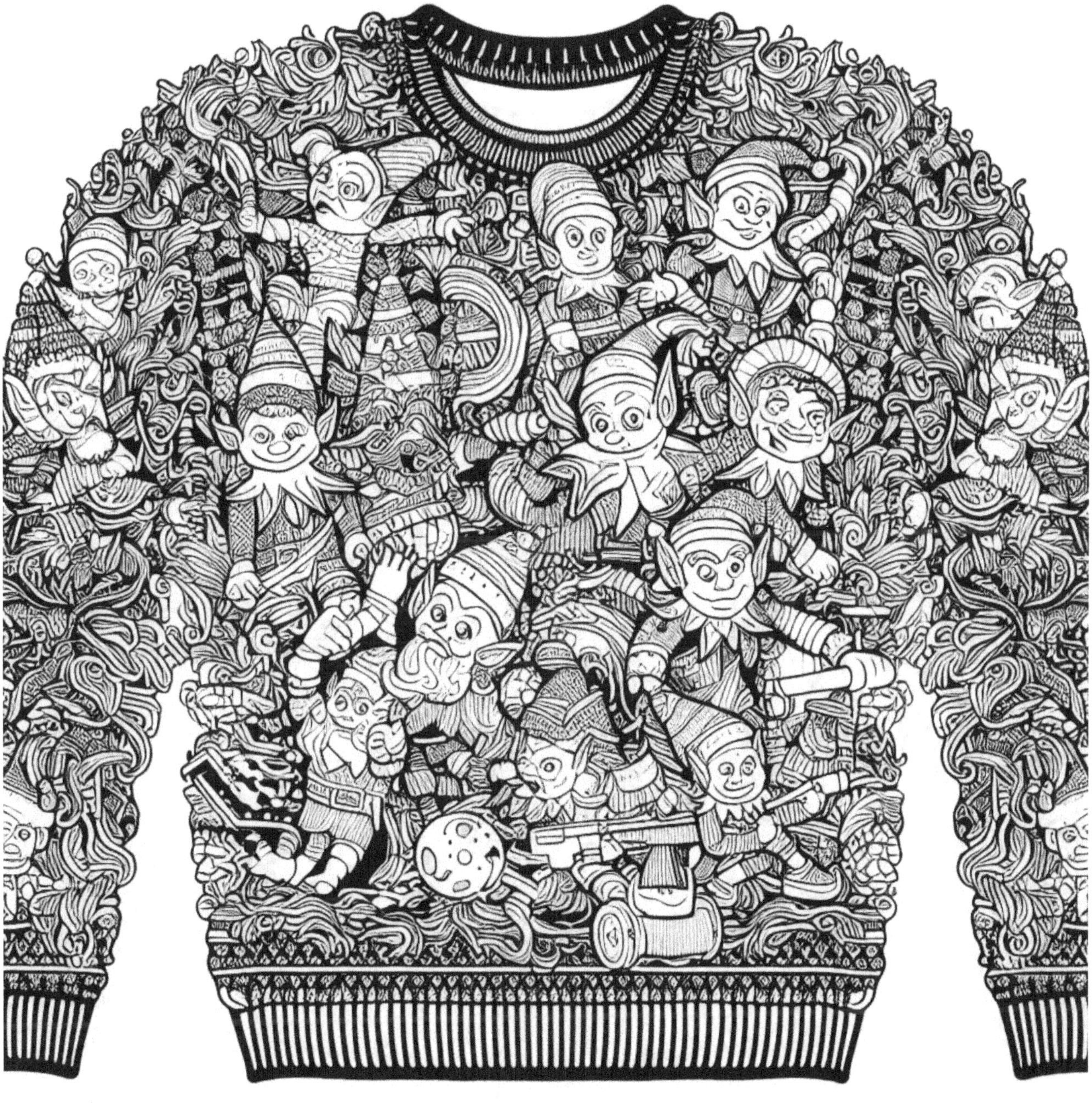

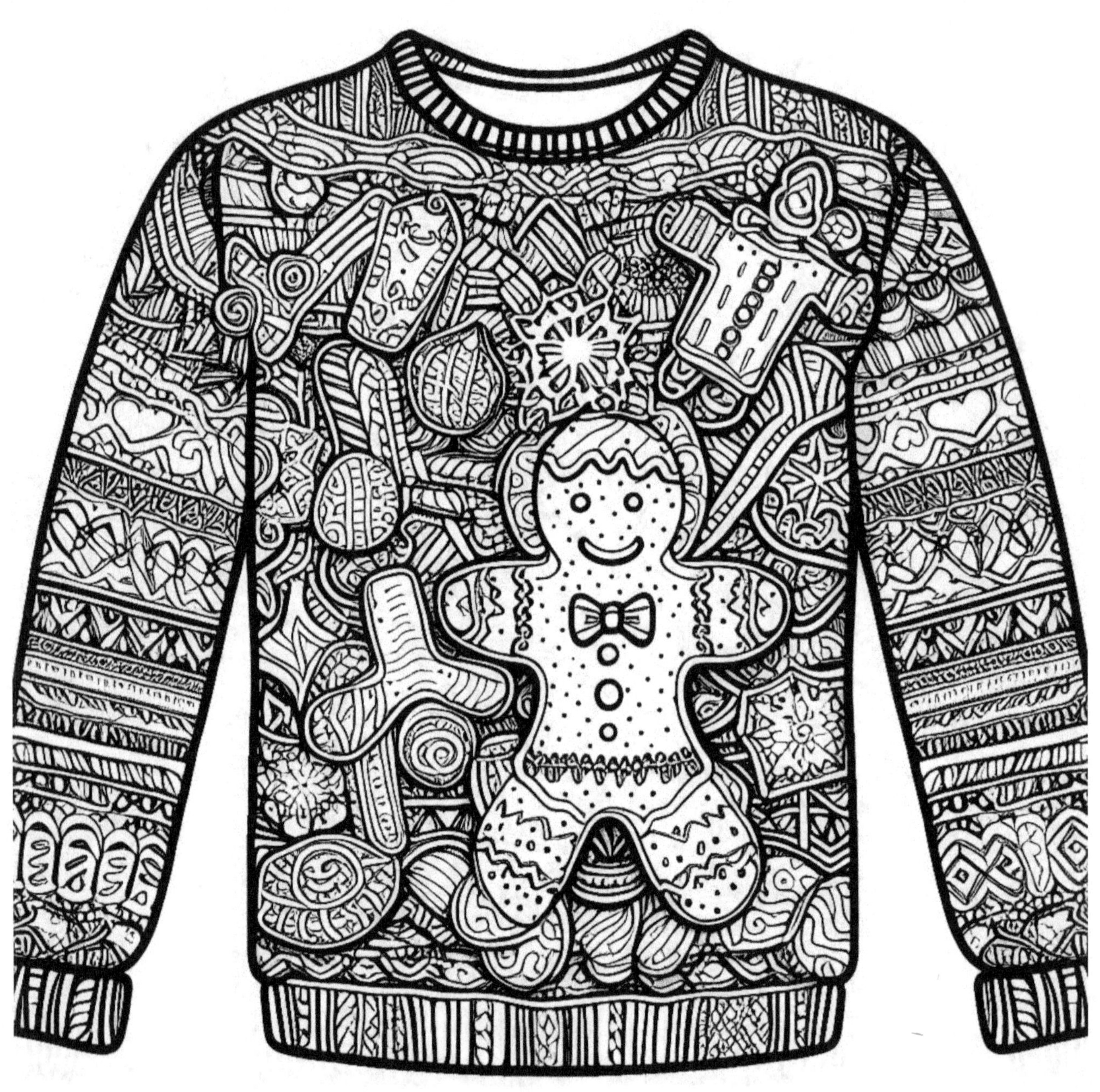

Gingerbread Wonderland

Welcome to "Ugly Sweater Christmas: A Festive Coloring Experience"!

This coloring book celebrates the whimsical and joyous tradition of the infamous ugly Christmas sweater. As you delve into these pages, get ready to embrace the holiday spirit in all its colorful, cozy, and delightfully tacky glory.

Embracing the Ugly Sweater Tradition

Ugly Christmas sweaters have evolved from fashion faux pas to a beloved and cherished part of holiday celebrations. These often garish, sometimes outrageous, and always festive sweaters have become an integral part of seasonal merriment, symbolizing a playful and lighthearted approach to the most wonderful time of the year.

Journey Through Tradition and Creativity

In this book, discover a variety of intricate and charming designs inspired by classic and quirky ugly sweater patterns. Unleash your creativity as you color these pages, bringing to life the intricate details and vibrant charm of these holiday-themed illustrations.

Celebration of Creativity and Relaxation

Coloring isn't just a fun activity—it's a way to unwind, de-stress, and express your creativity. Dive into the world of holiday cheer, intricate patterns, and festive scenes that will transport you to a cozy and imaginative space, allowing you to embrace the essence of the season in a uniquely personal way.

Let Your Imagination Run Wild

Whether you're an avid coloring enthusiast or a novice looking for a creative escape, this book is designed to engage, inspire, and encourage your imagination. Get ready to add your personal touch, experimenting with colors and bringing these ugly sweater designs to life in your own unique style.

Prepare to embark on a colorful journey filled with warmth, whimsy, and holiday cheer. So grab your favorite coloring tools, immerse yourself in the magic of the season, and let the festive coloring adventure begin!

Happy coloring and Merry Christmas!

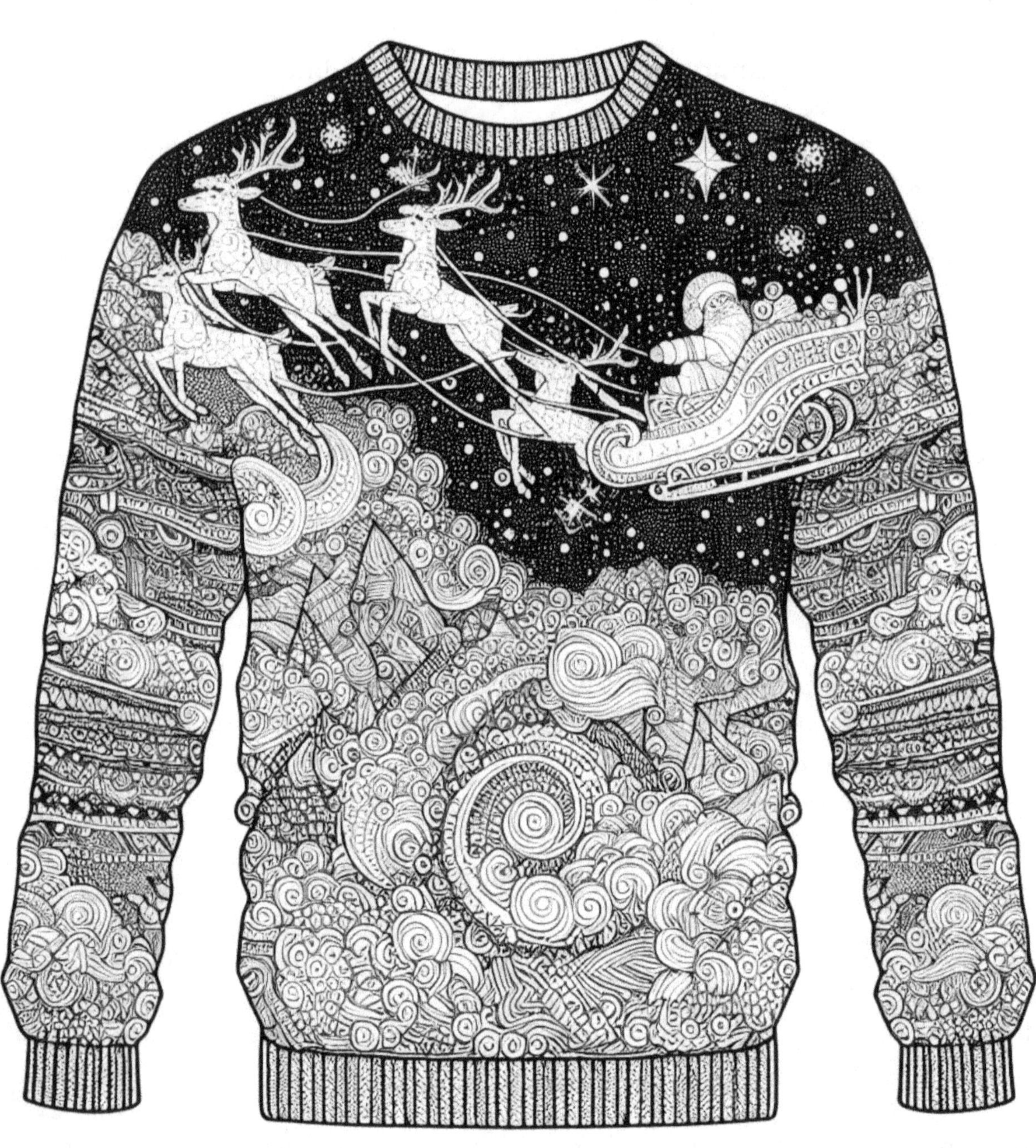

Santa's Sleigh Spectacle

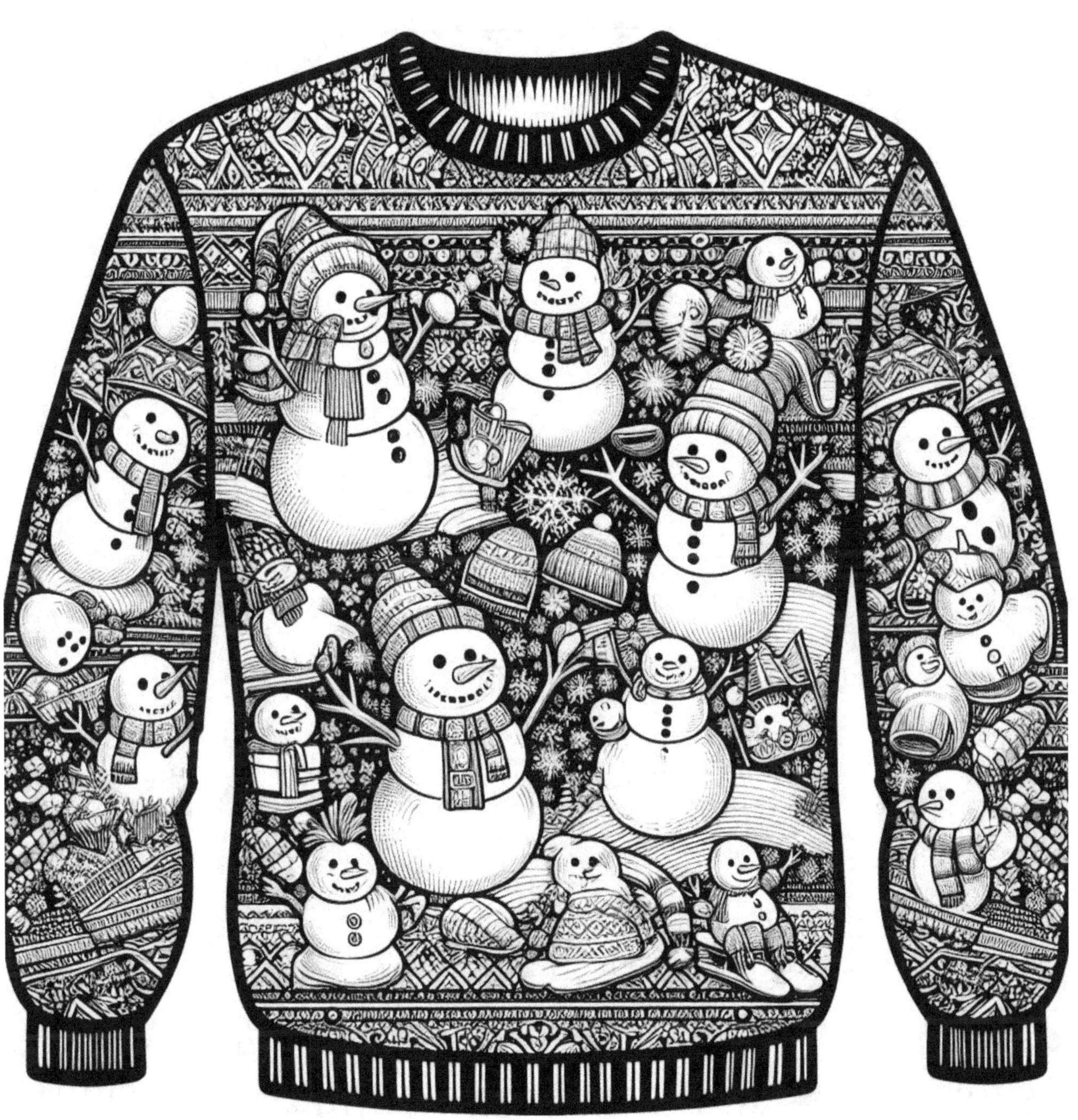

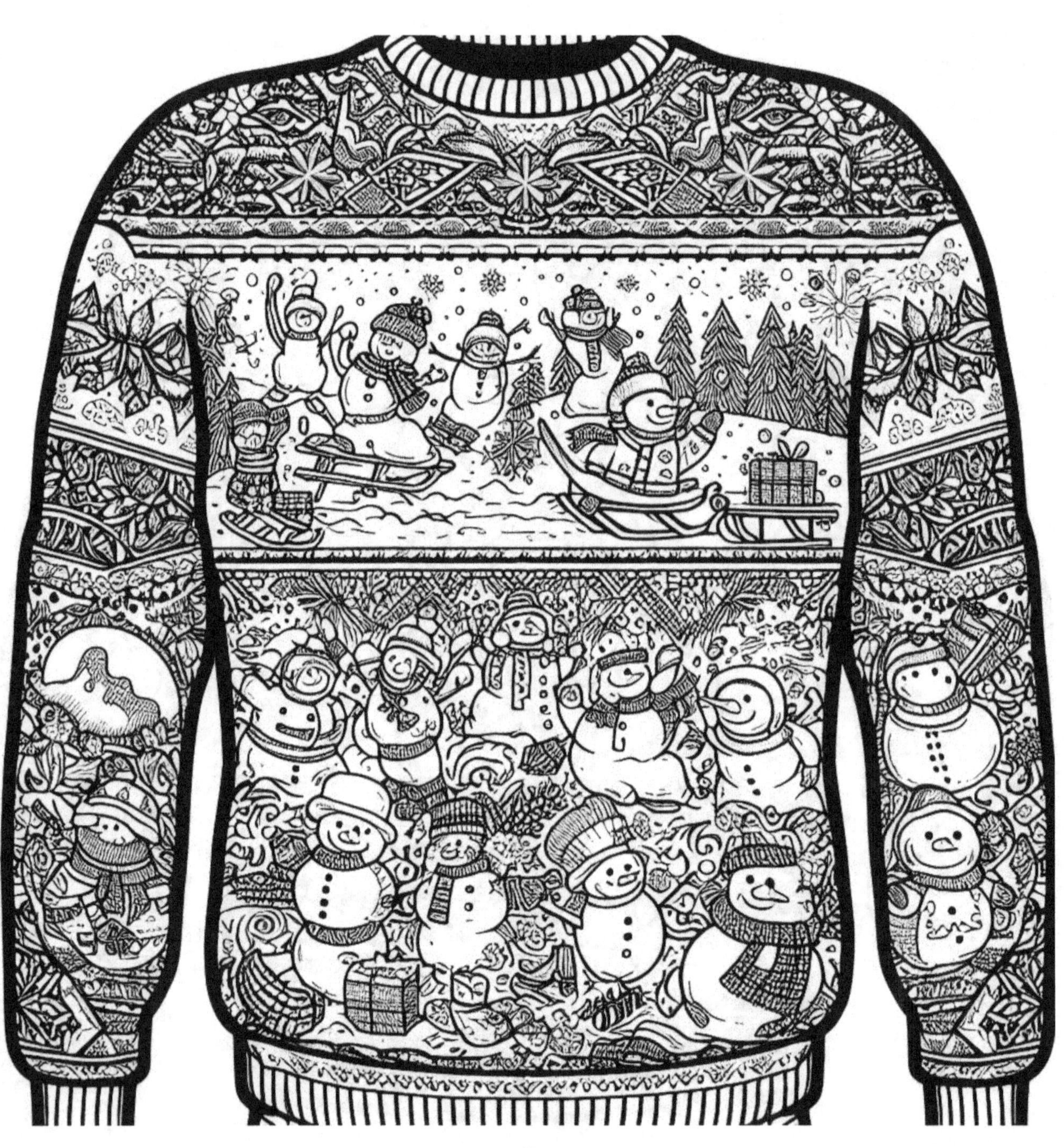

Festive Flora and Fauna

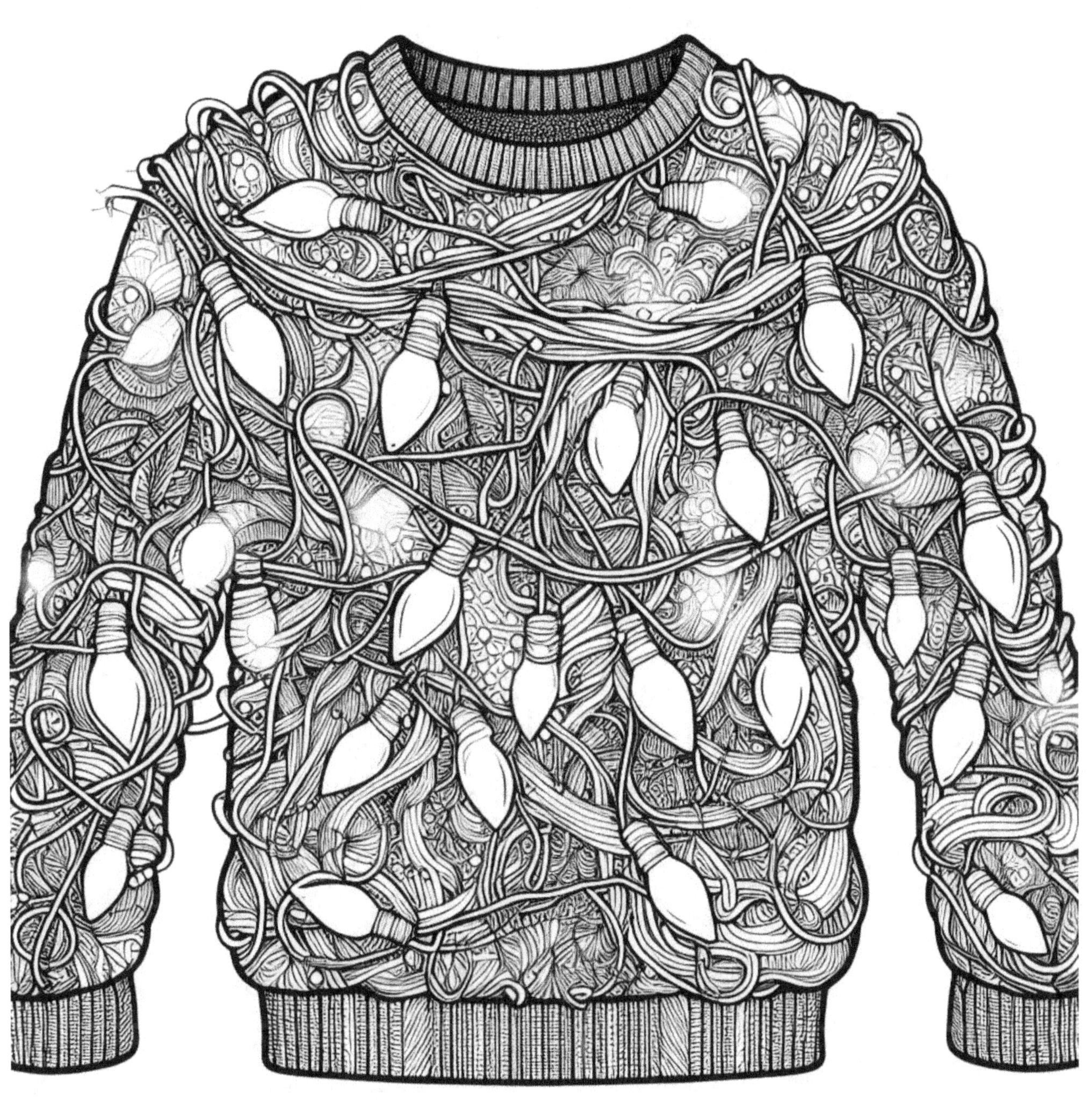
Christmas Lights Galore

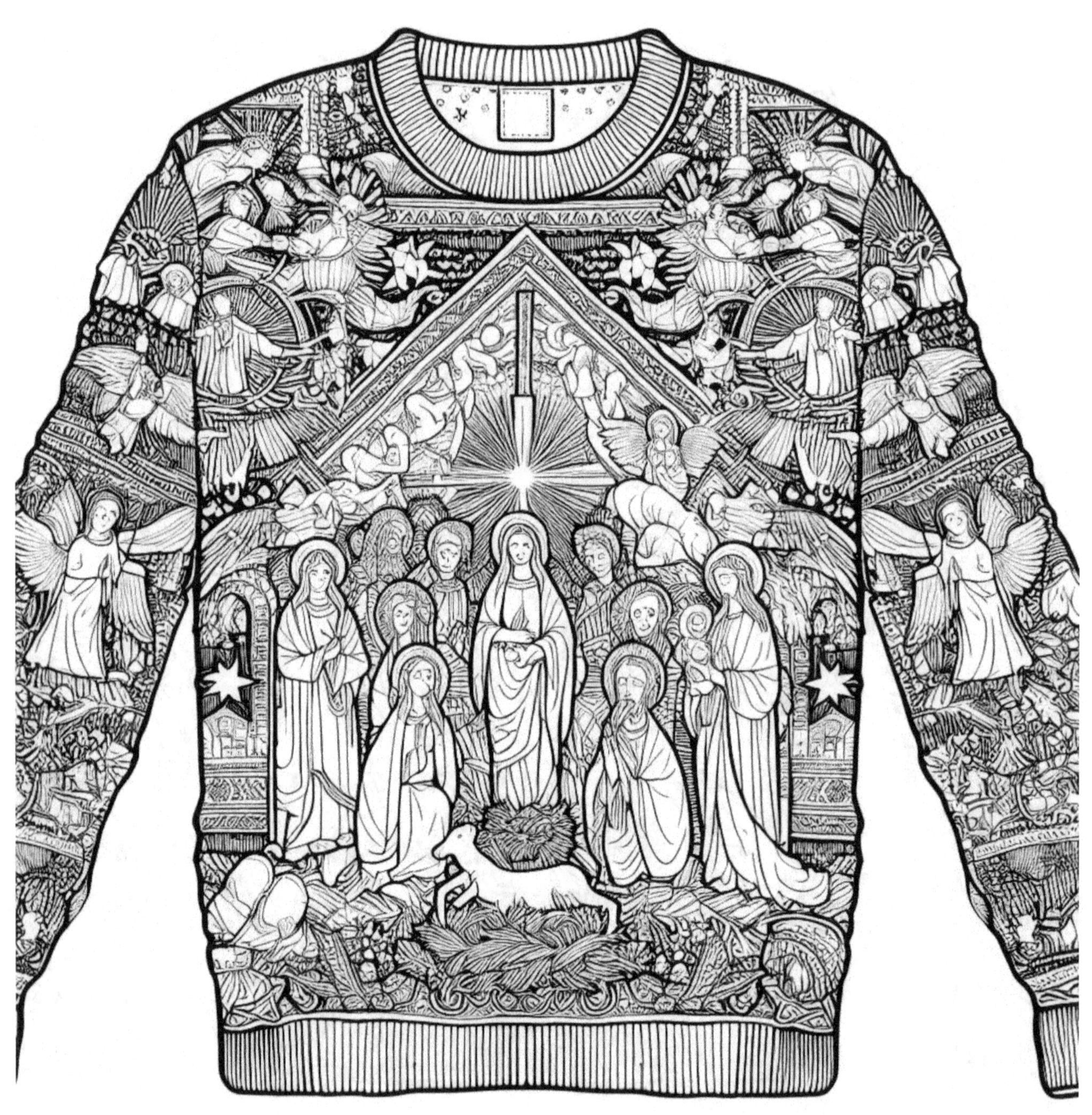

Ugly Sweater Nativity

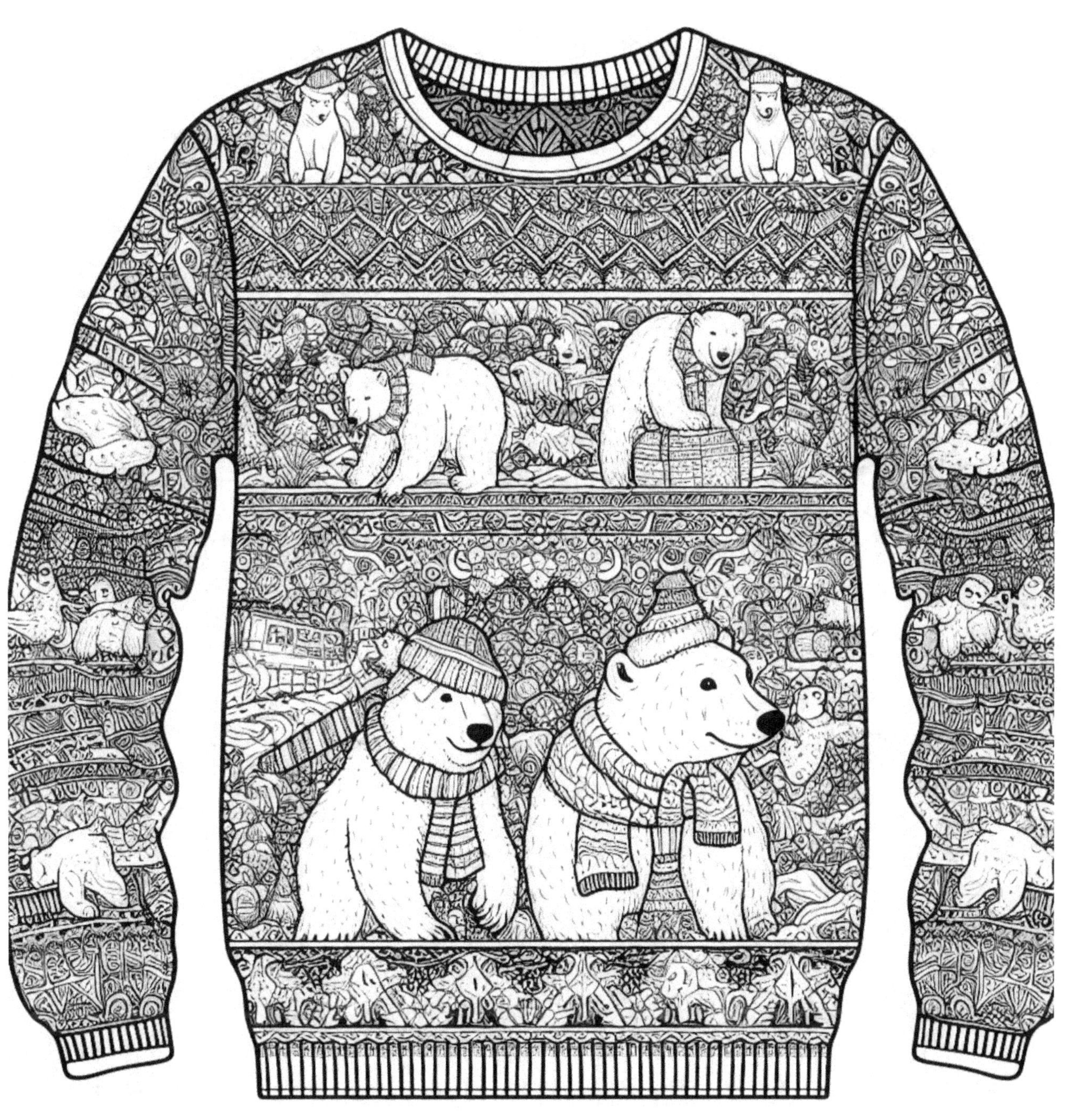

Polar Bear Party

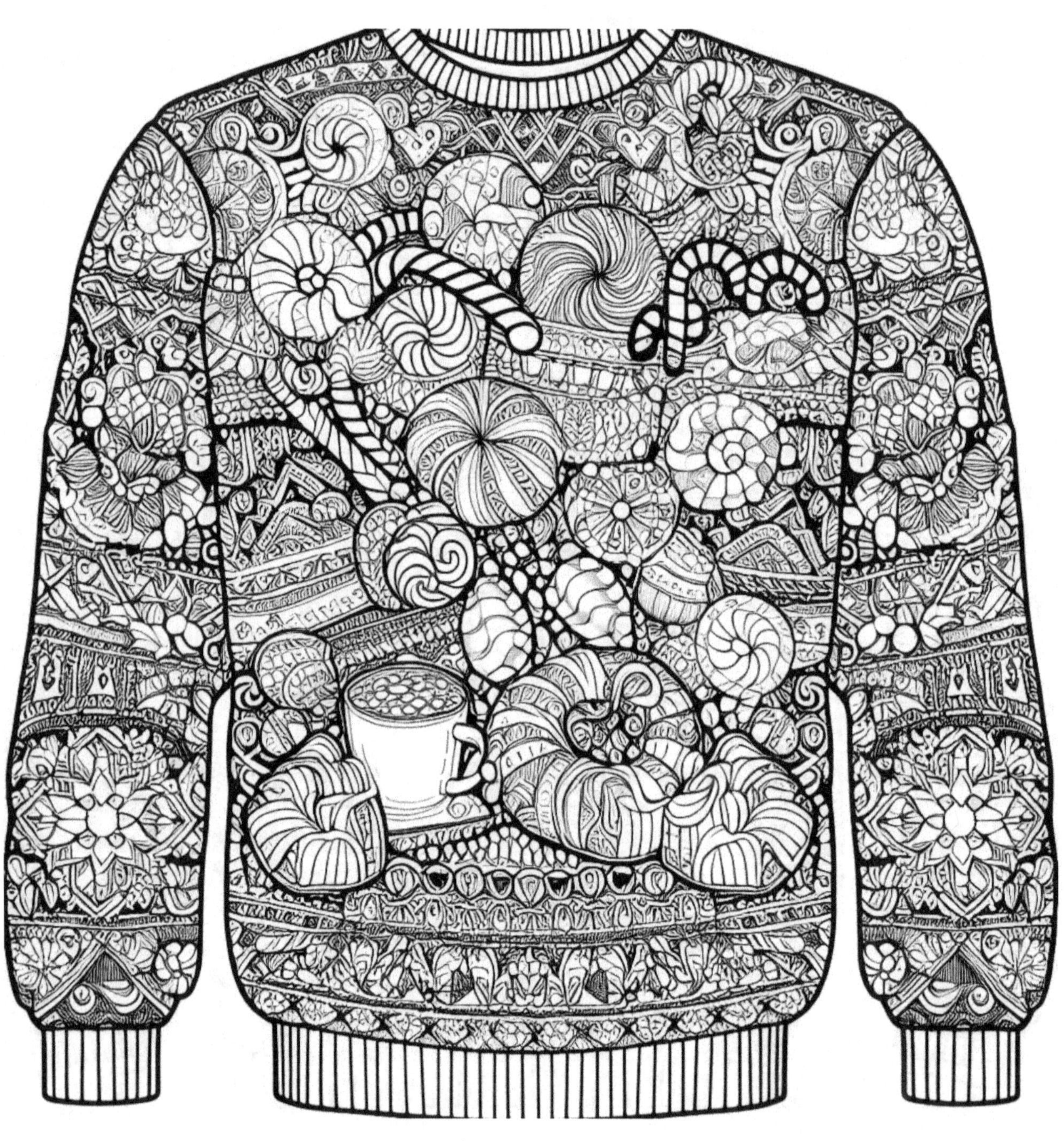

Holiday Treats Fiesta

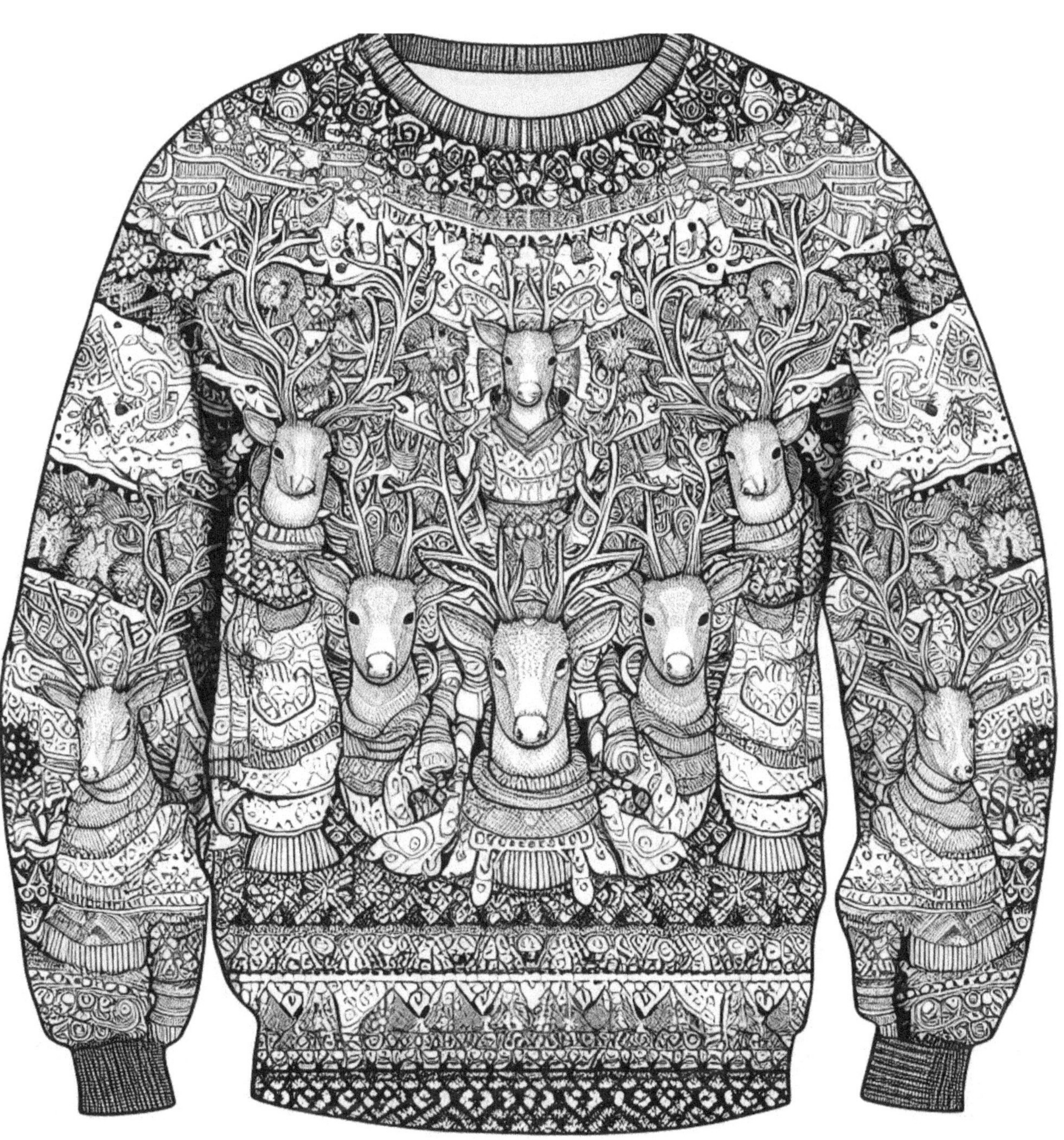
Reindeer Rampage

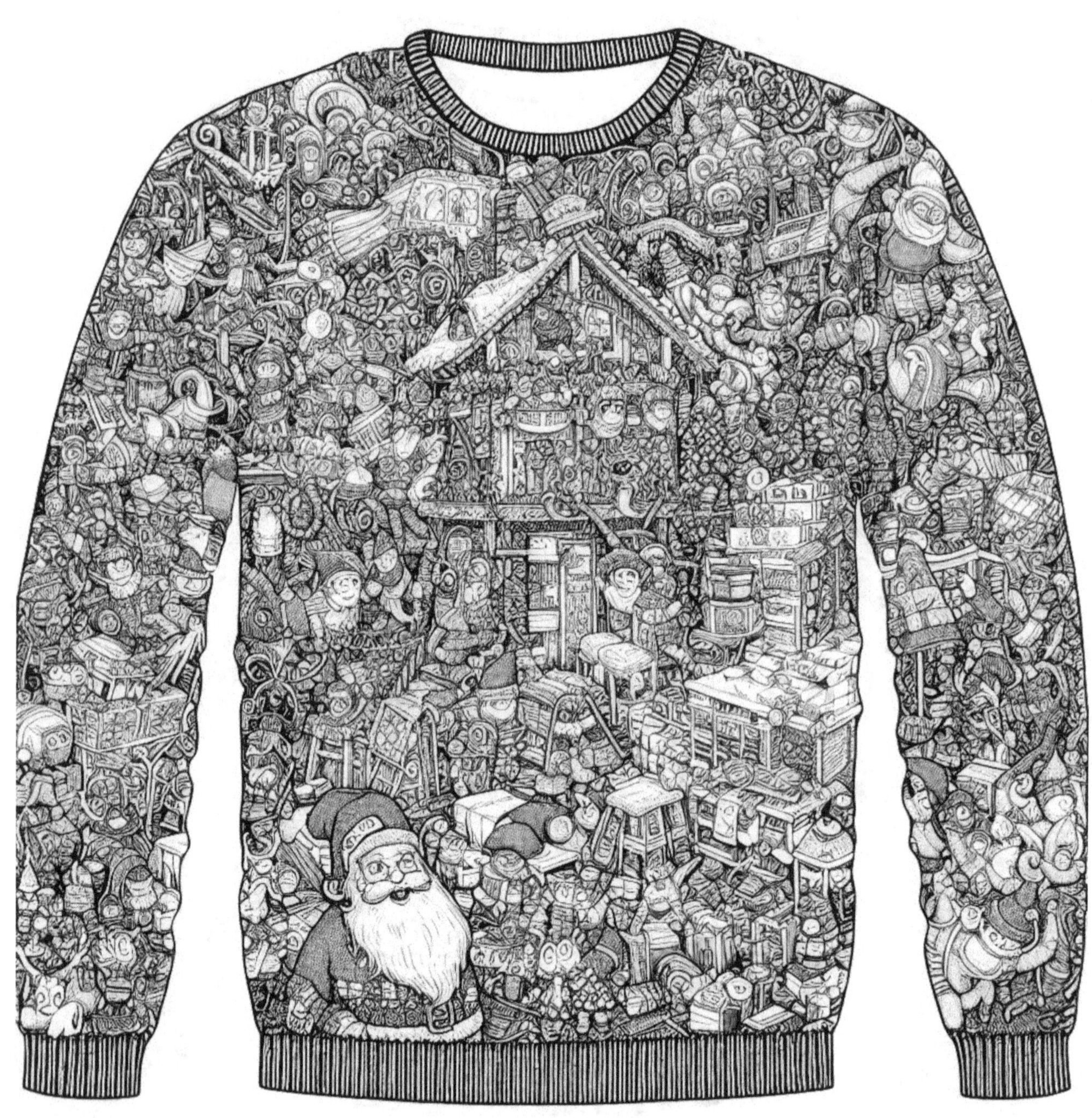

North Pole Chaos

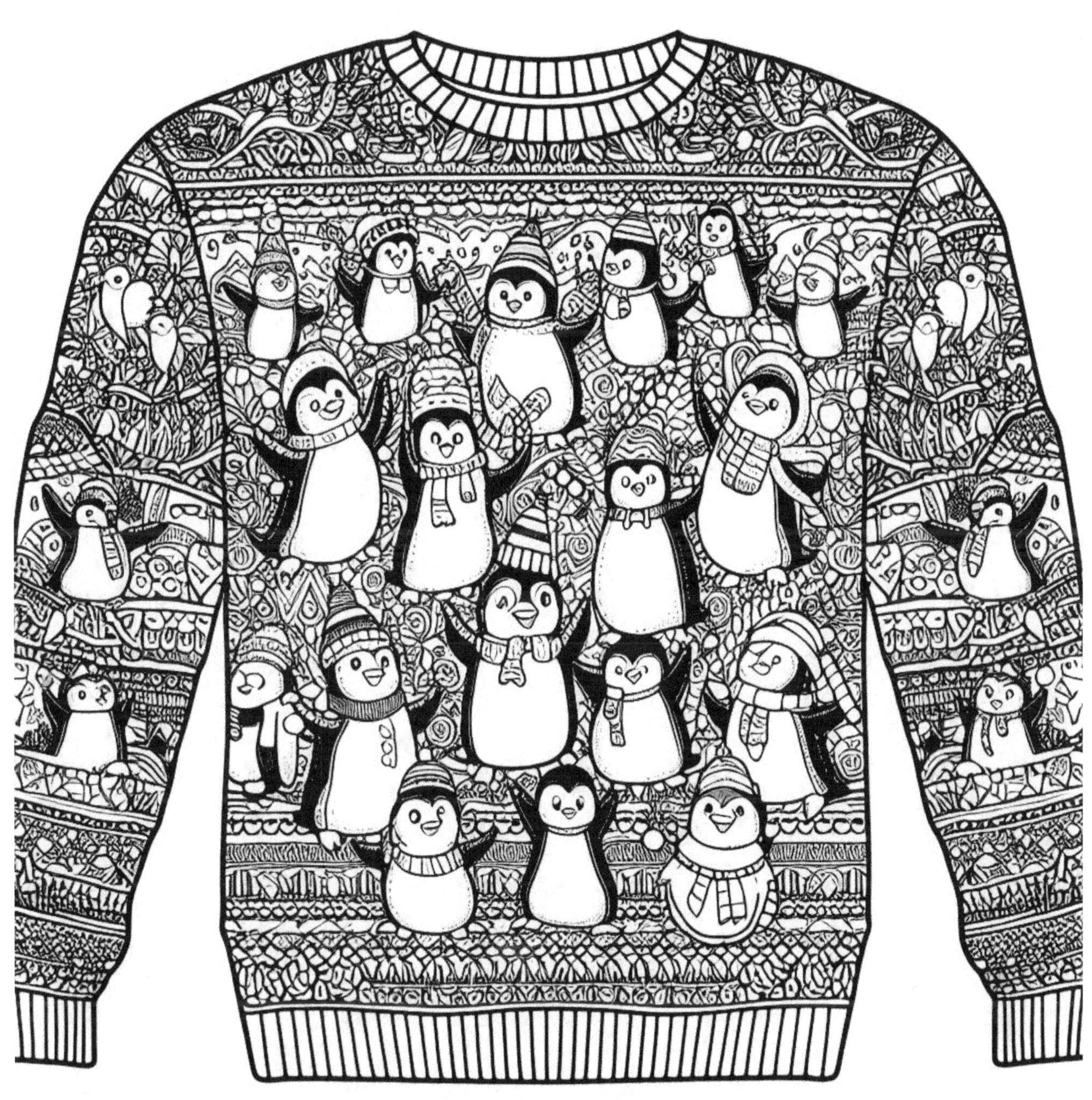

Penguin Parade

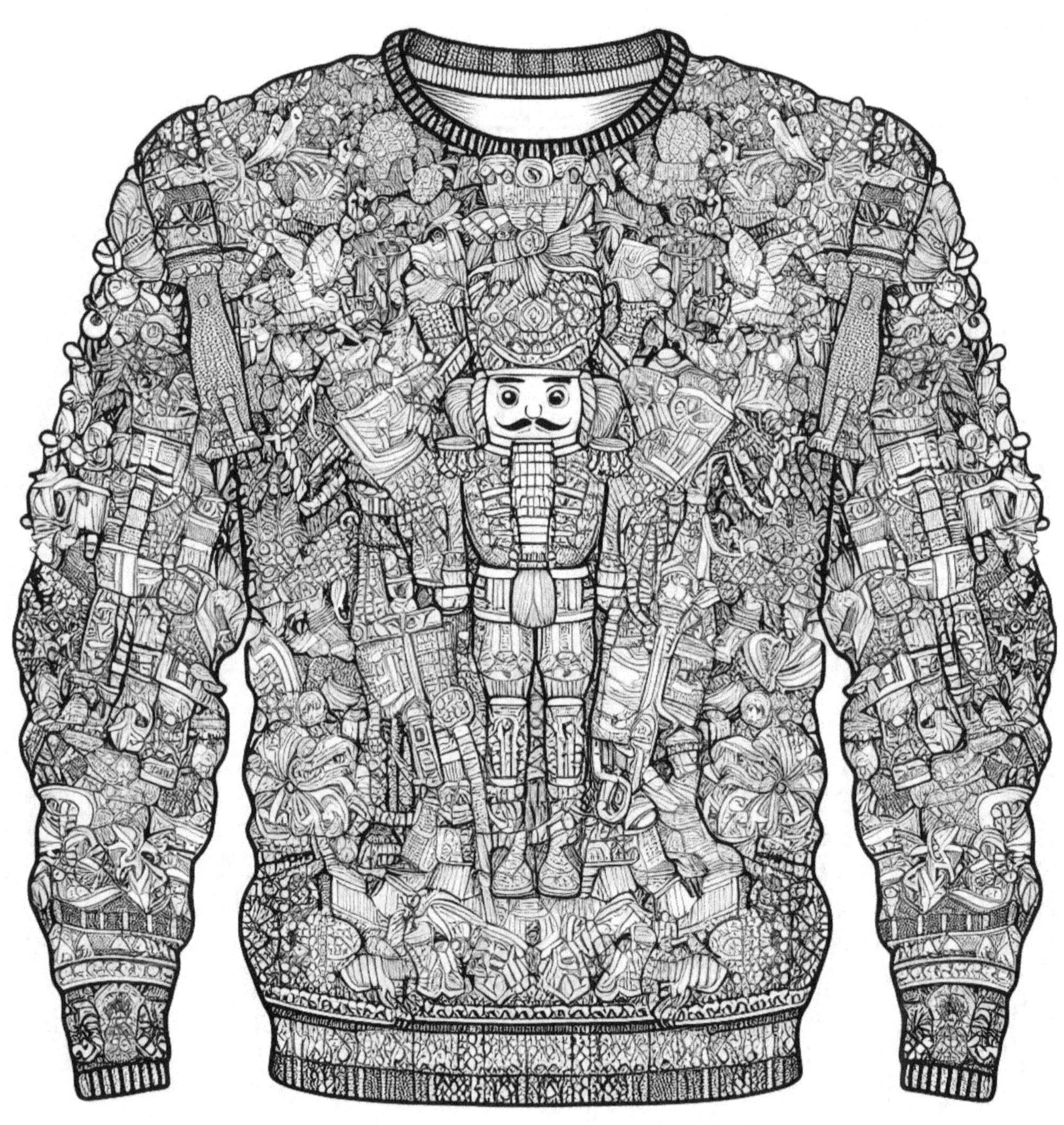

Nutcracker Nonsense

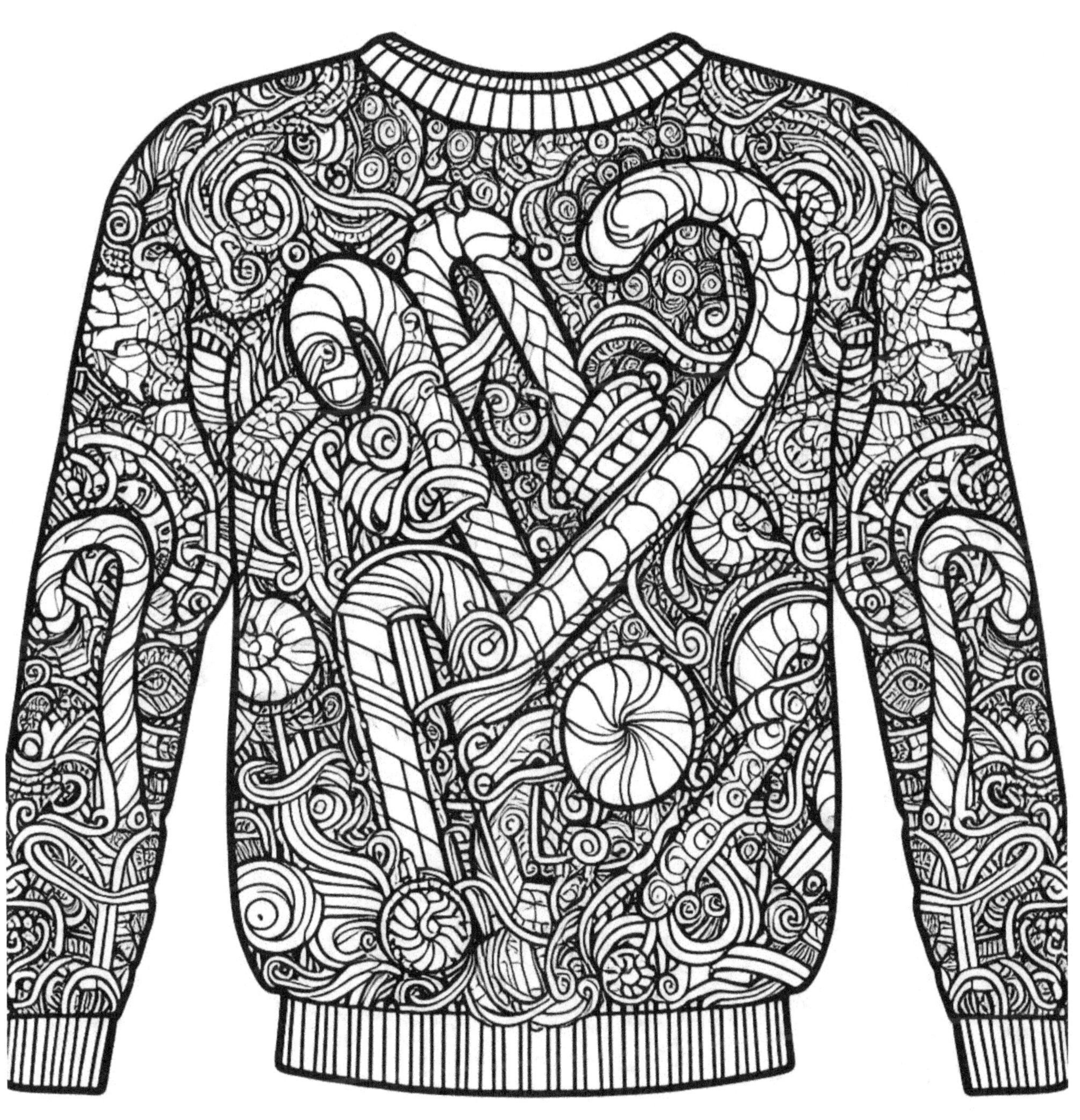
Candy Cane Catastrophe

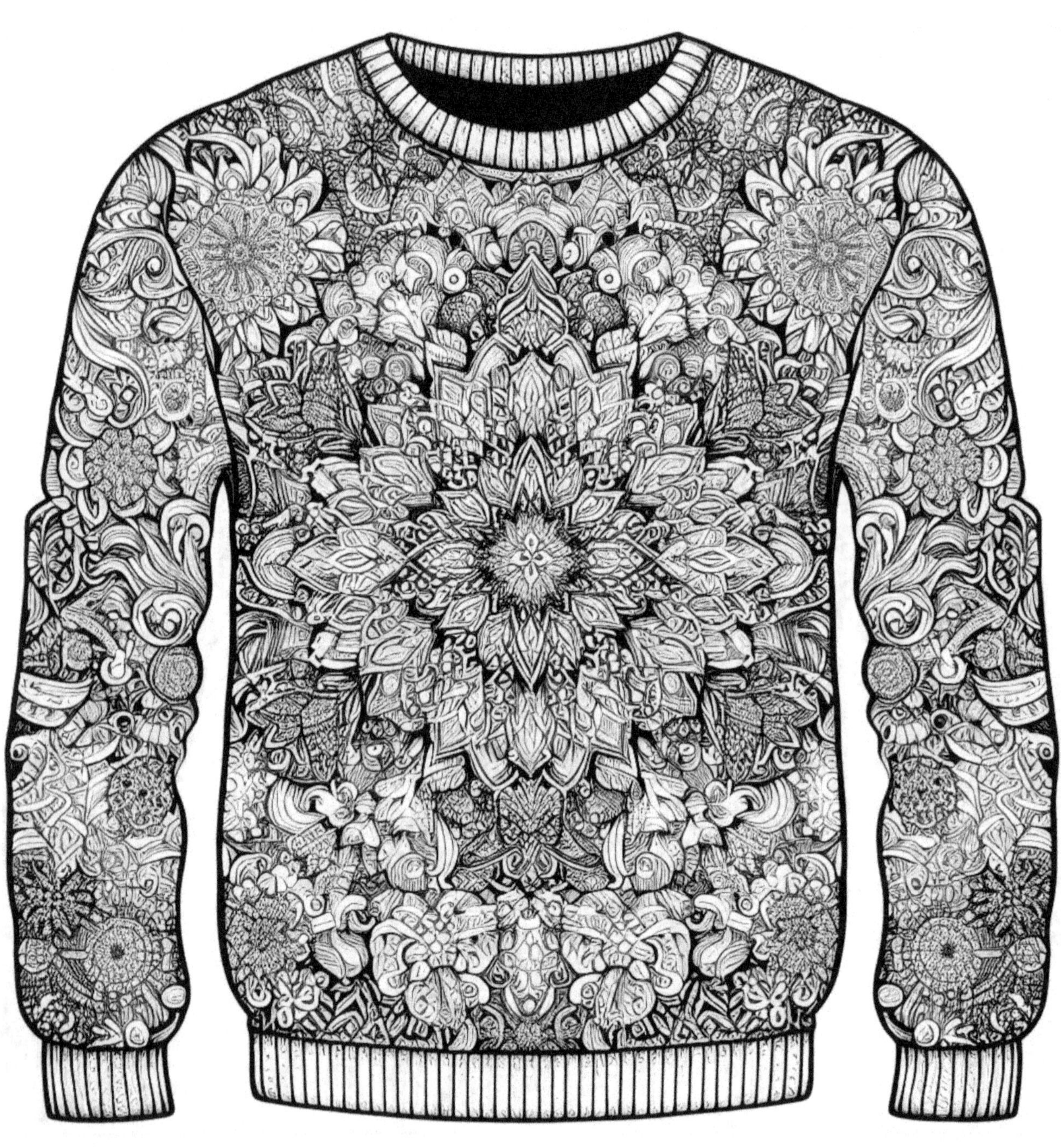

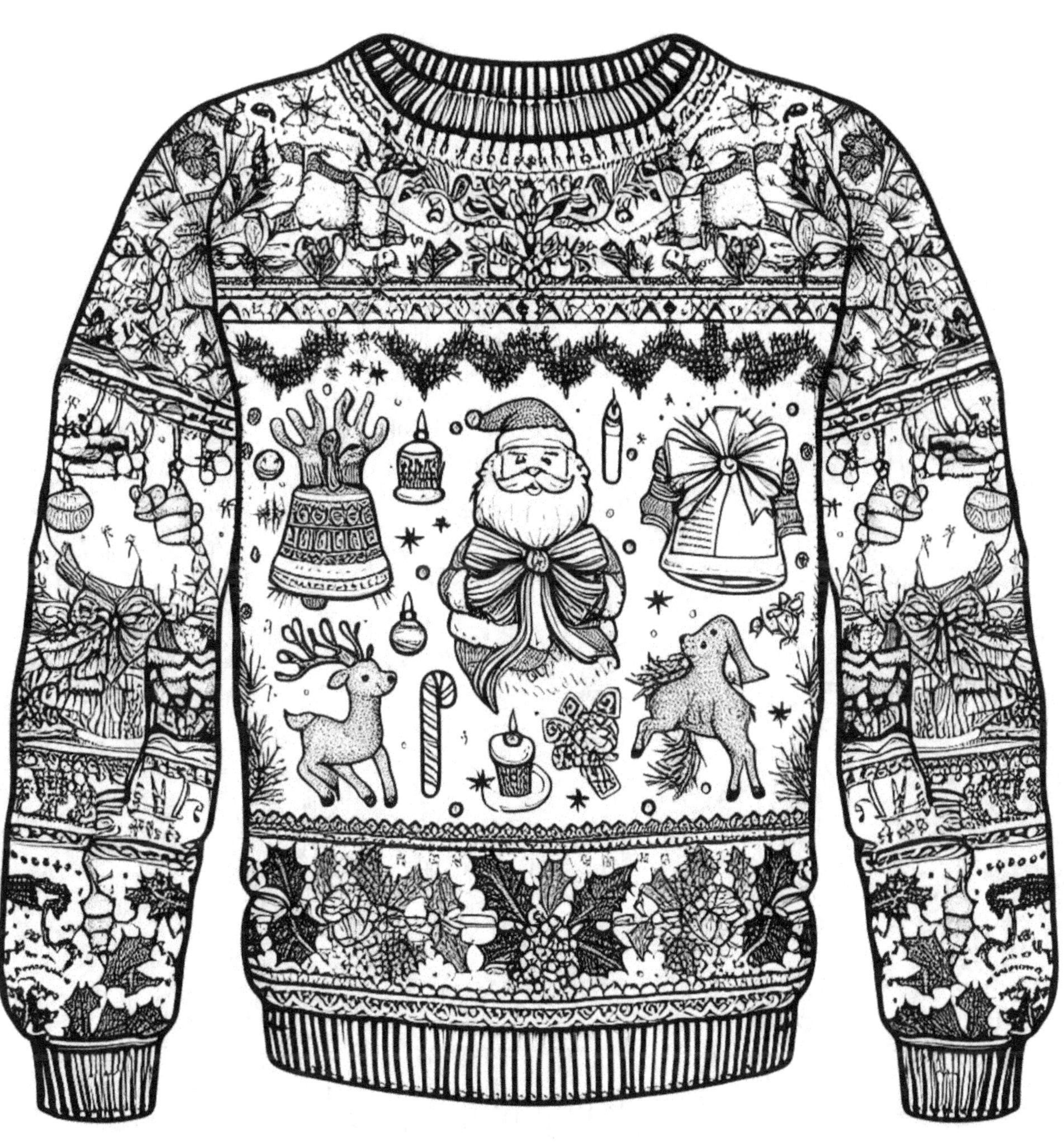

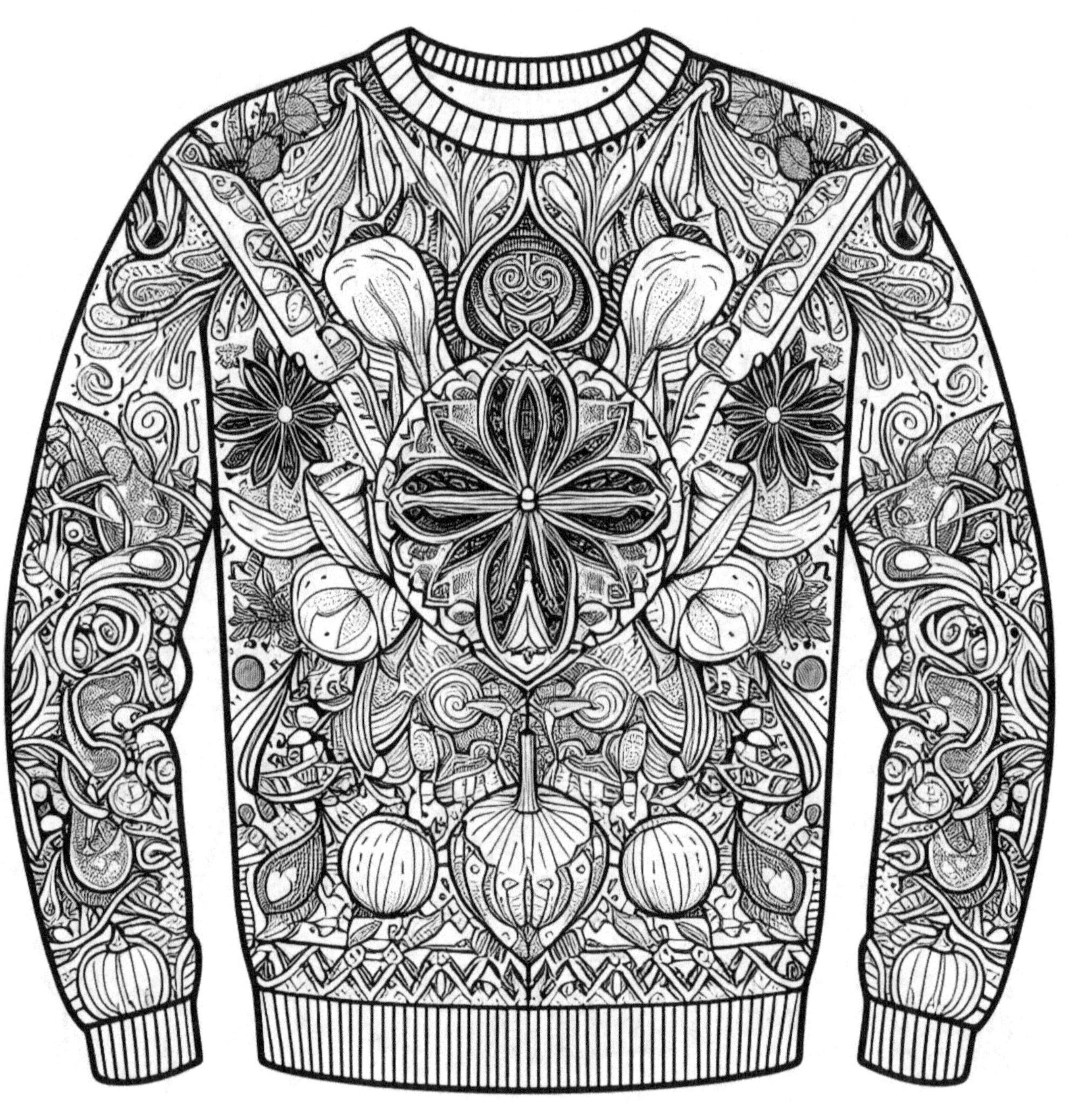

Magical Nutmeg

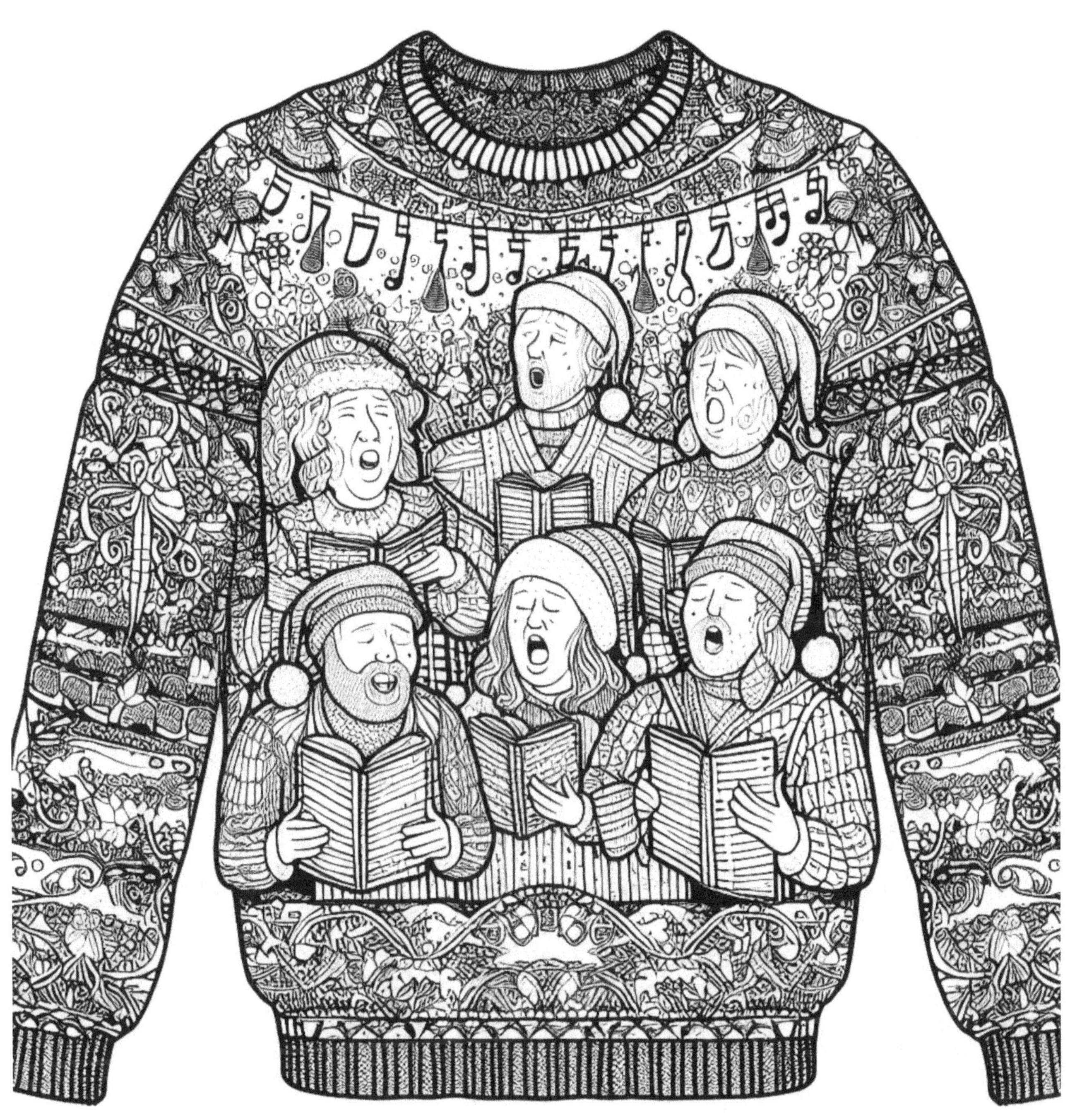

Carolers' Carnival

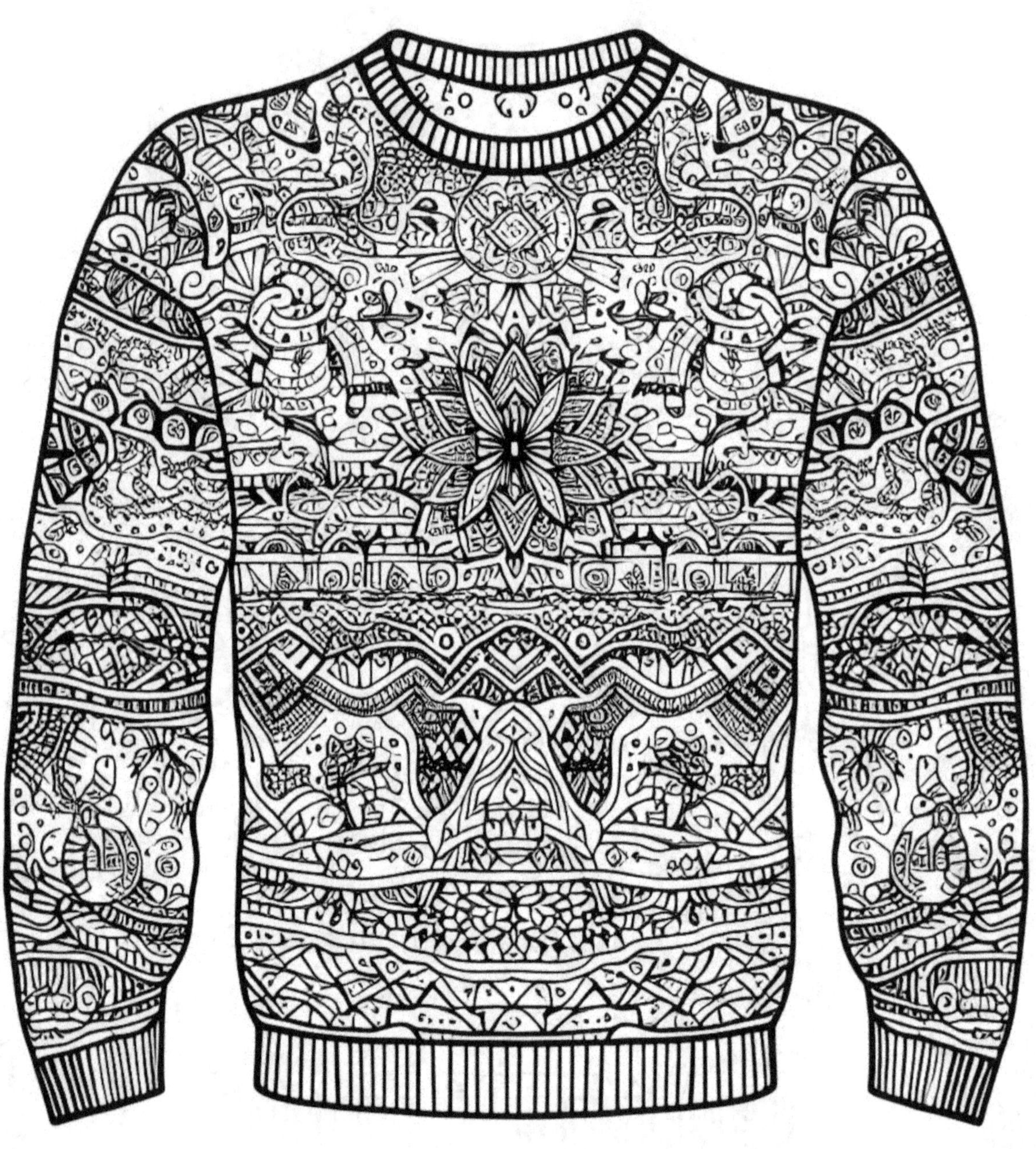

Winter Whirlwind

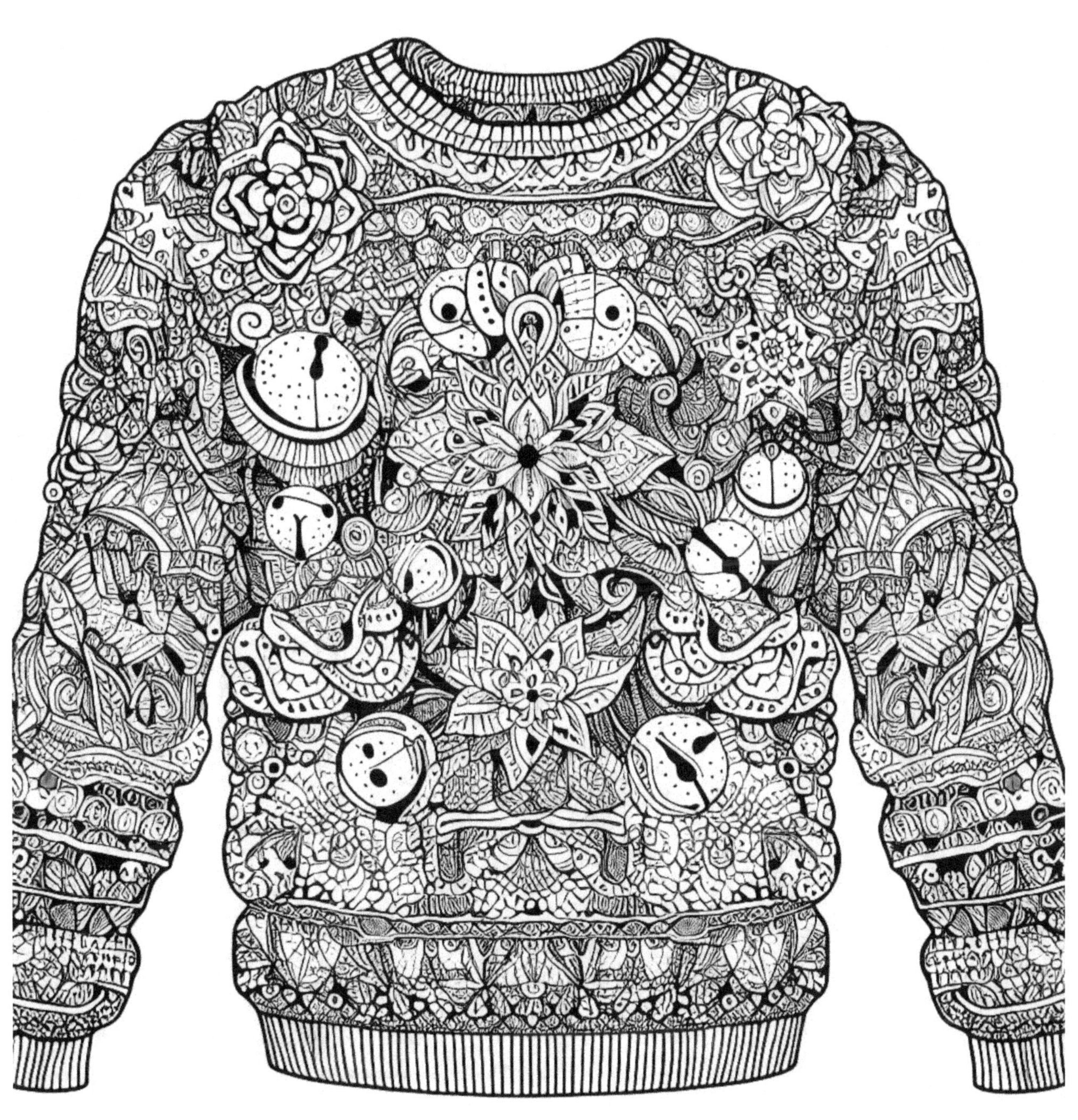

Jovial Jingle Bells

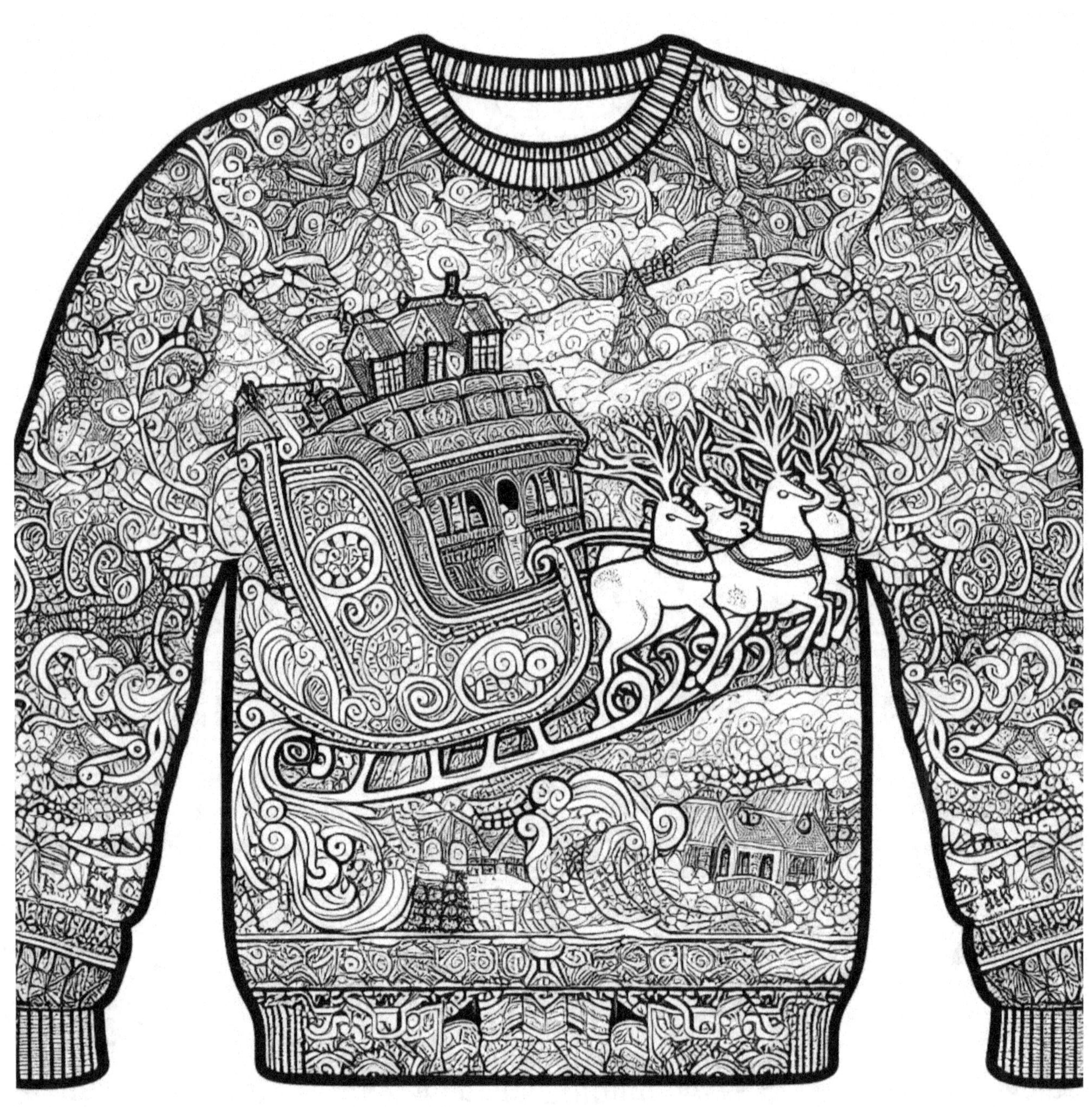

Santa's Sleigh

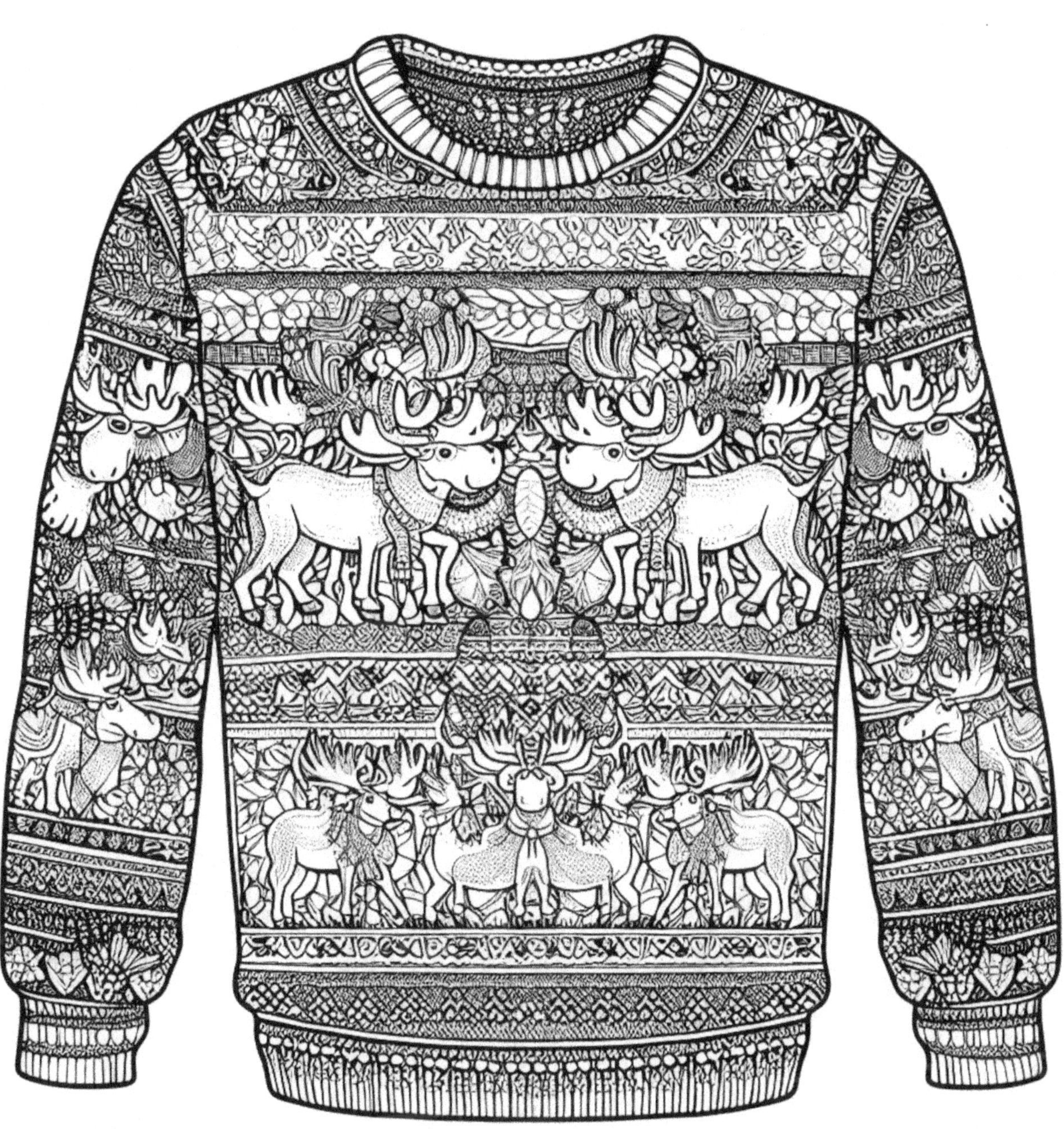

Merry Moose Christmas

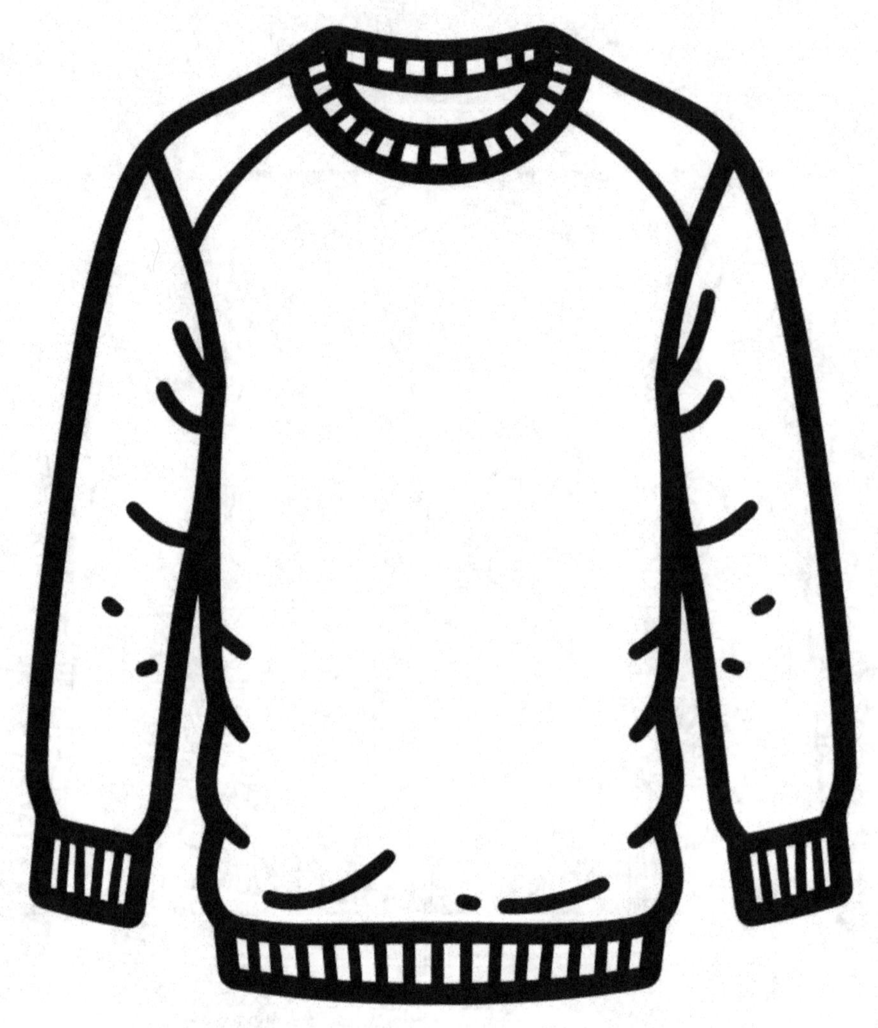

Create Your Own Ugly Sweater

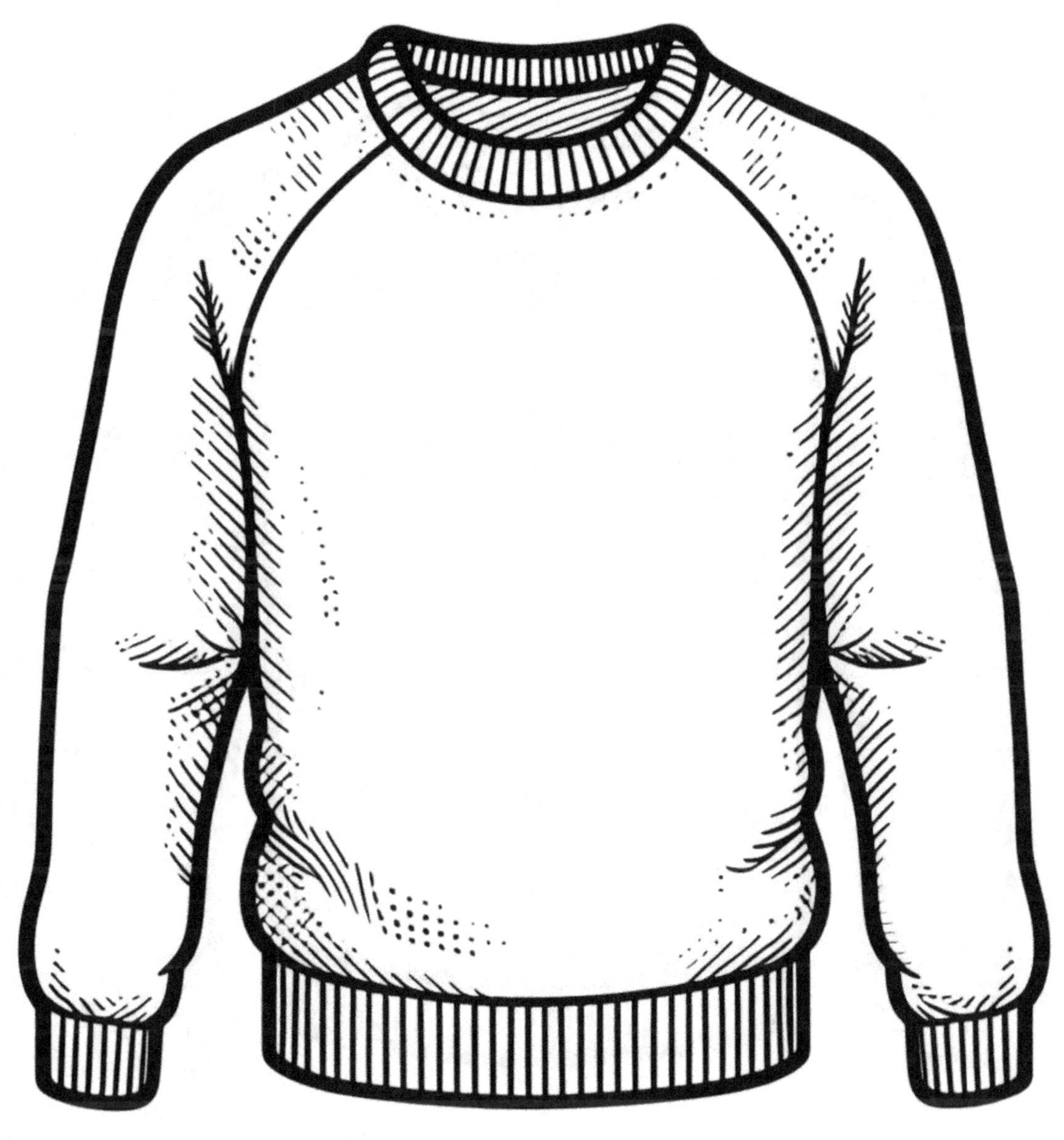

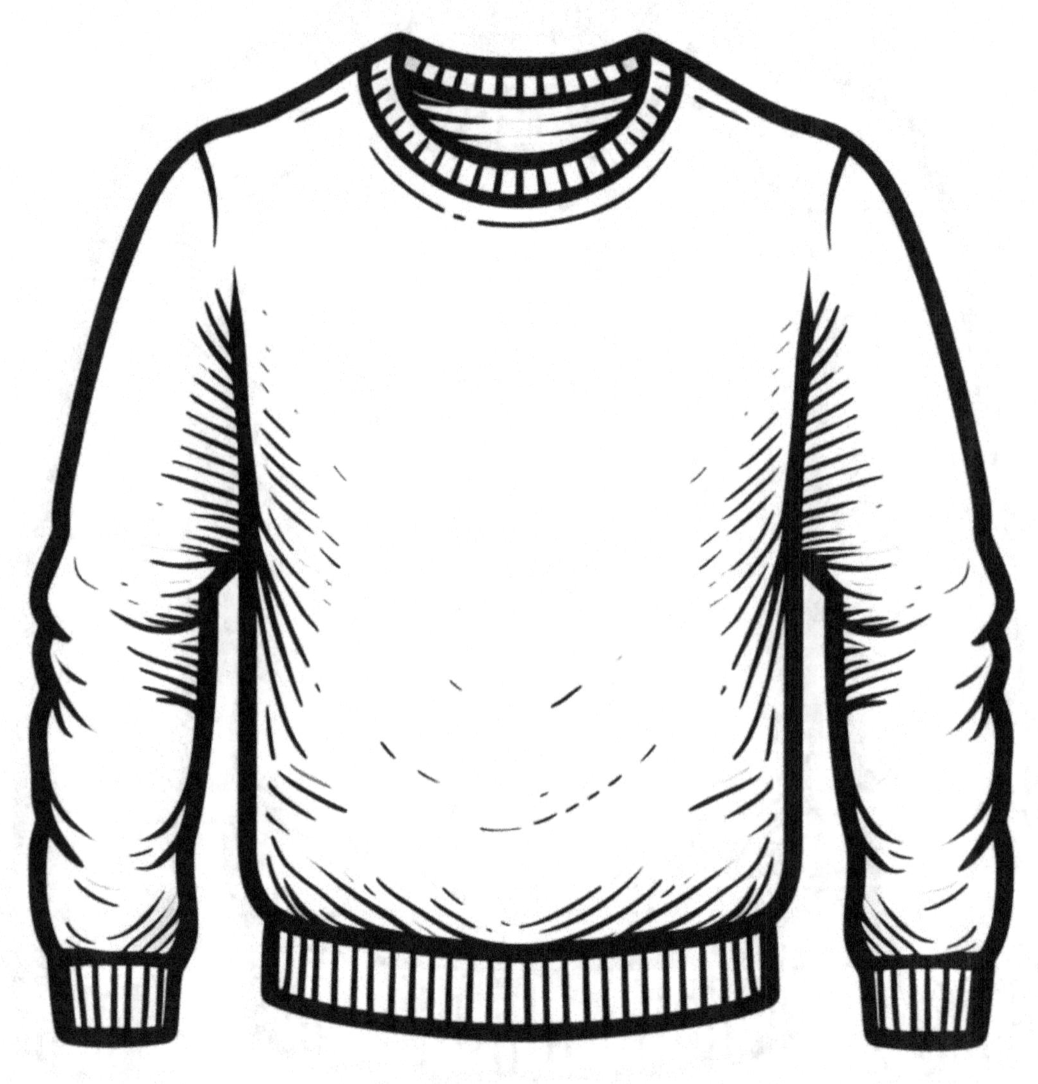

Create Your Own Ugly Sweater

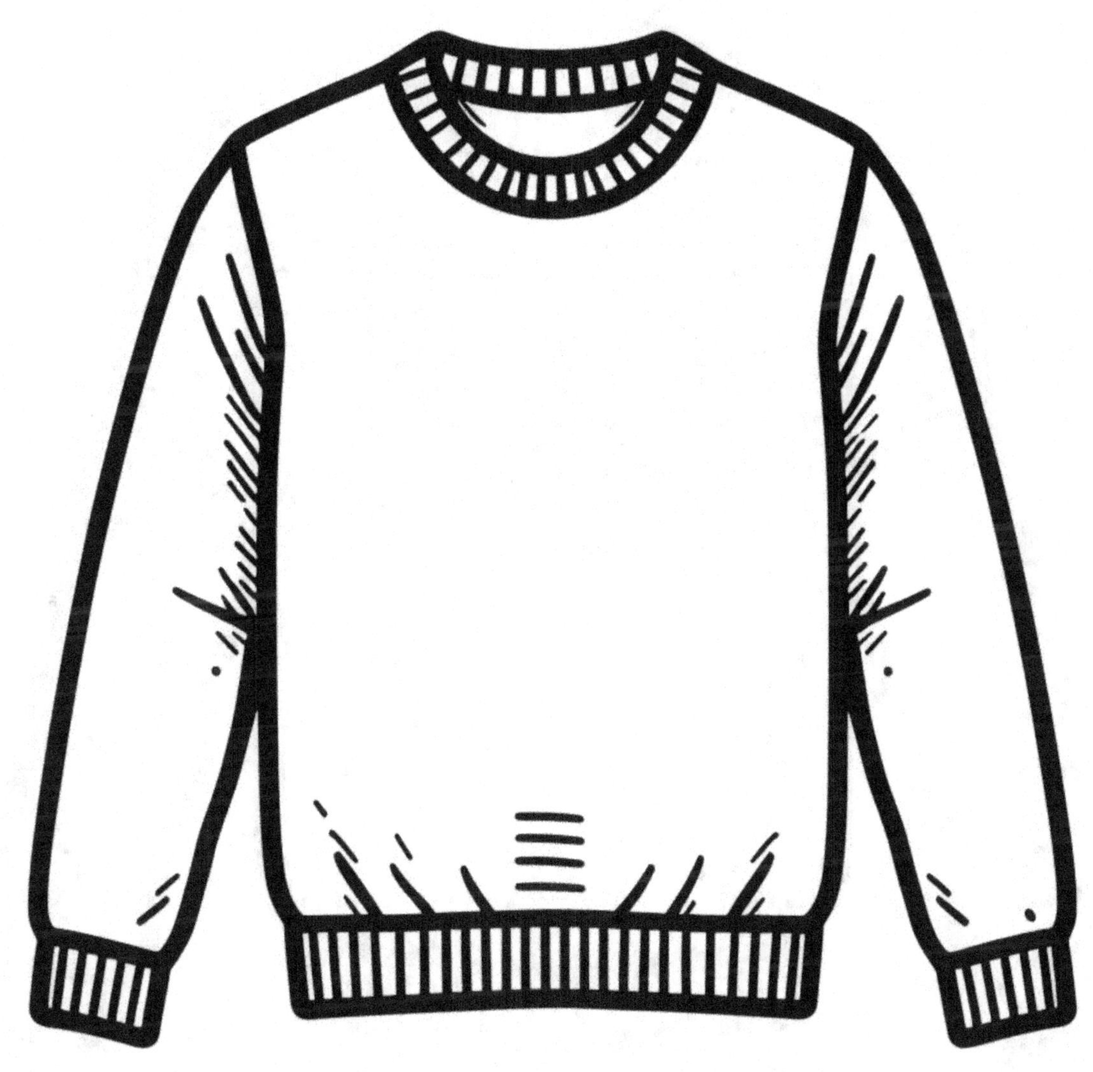
Create Your Own Ugly Sweater

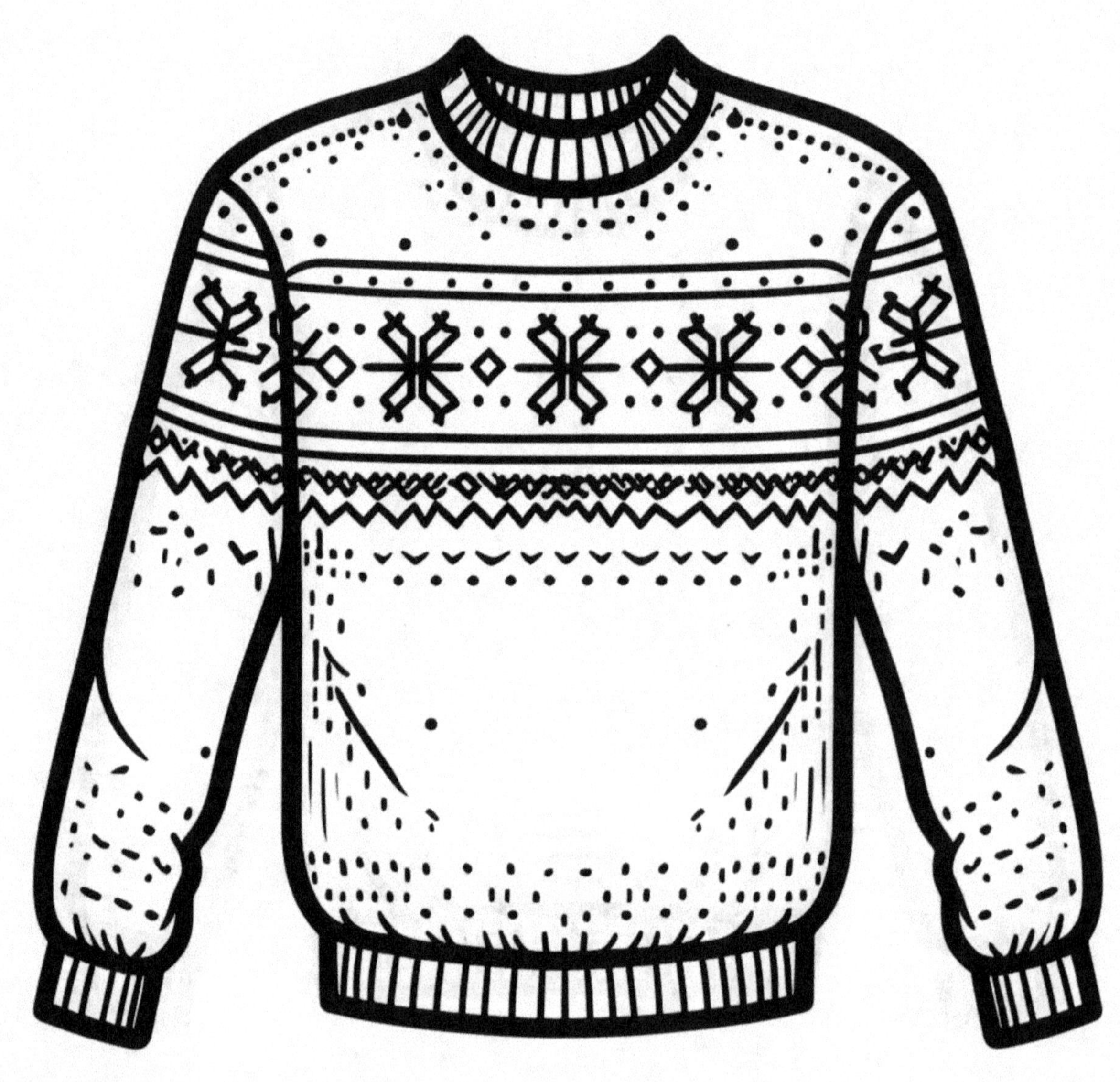

Create Your Own Ugly Sweater

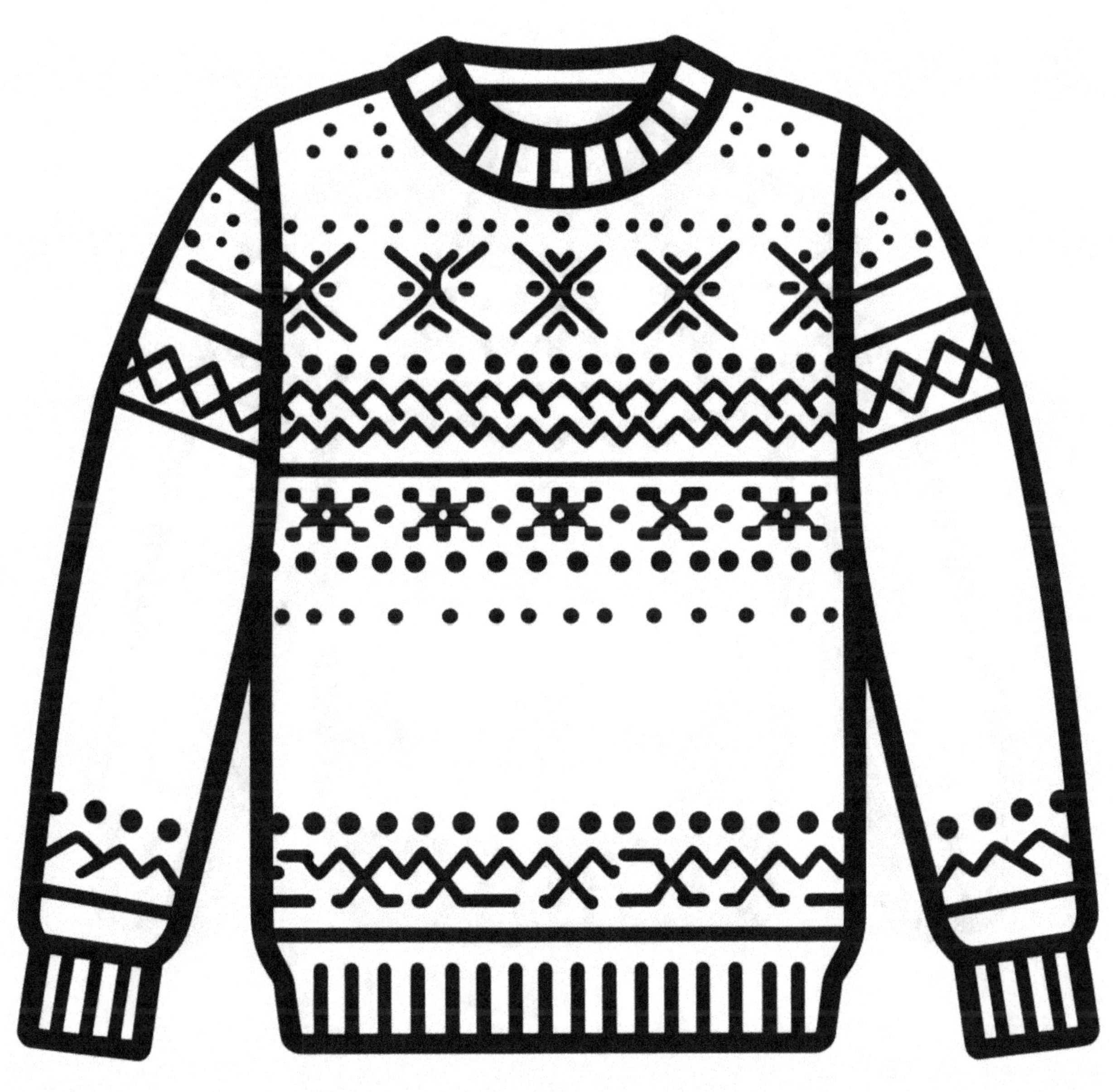
Create Your Own Ugly Sweater

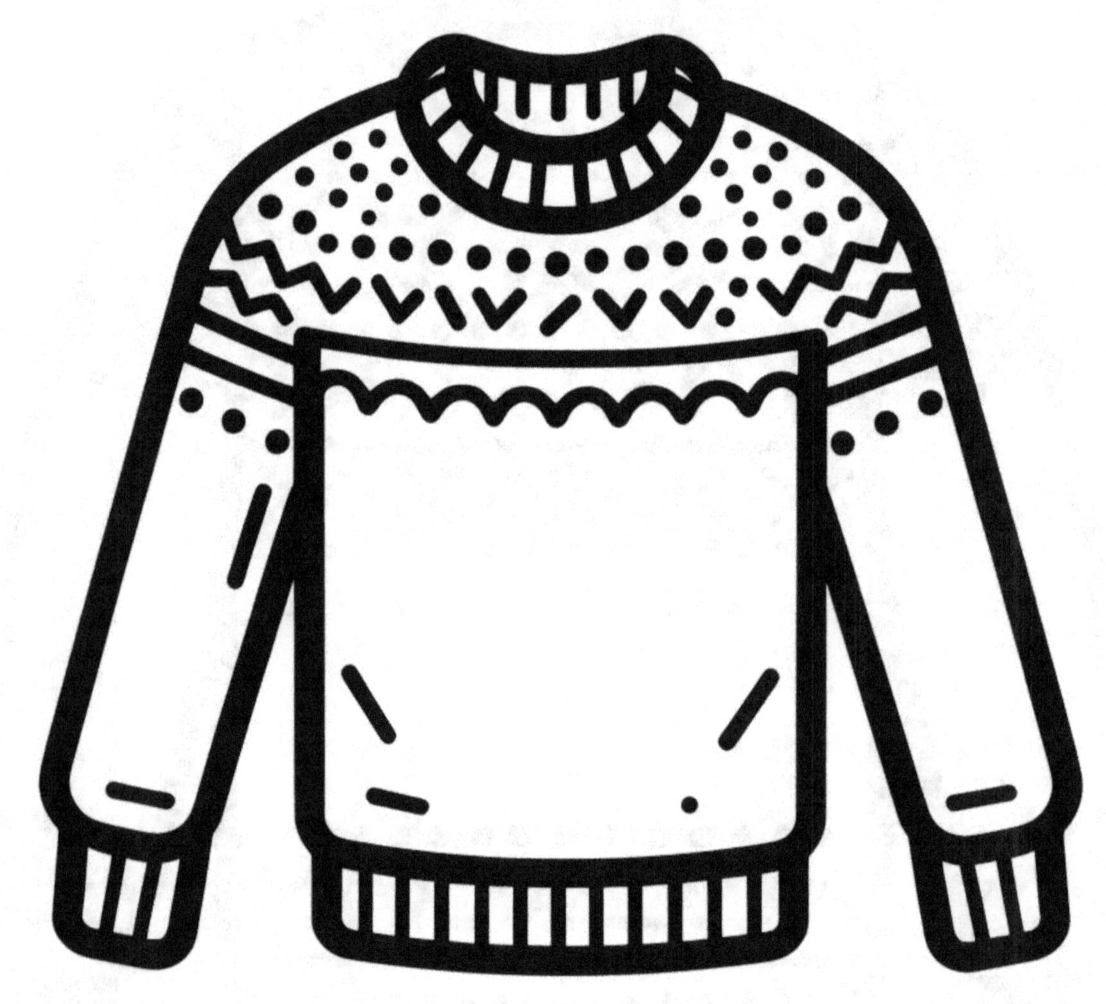

Create Your Own Ugly Sweater